Acknowledgements:

I would like to thank Ms. Felene Cayetano,

National Heritage Library for the commitment to literature and

her valuable assistance in getting my manuscript to print.

Thank you Mrs. Joy Ysaguirre, Chief librarian (retired) for your

encouragement, counsel and friendship.

To my wife Jillanna Crawford
and my sons Ezequiel, Jemuel, Ryan and David

Creole Bread

My mother makes Creole bread
Great! Creole bread!
On the creaky wooden kitchen table
Near the window
With the blinds shut to keep the cool
In the room and the conkas out

My mother makes Creole bread
Great! Creole bread!
In the hand-craved mahogany bowl
The wood seasoned with grease and sweat
And the heat. She stands on her feet
She measures the flour by the size
Of the heap. Adds the salt and the
Brown sugar, with her hands, callous
By the heel of the palm where she kneads
The dough. She adds a bit more

My mother makes Creole bread
Great! Creole bread!
Mixing in the shortening
Pouring yeast like lava then
Coconut milk. Mixing with her hands
Keeping the wooden bowl in place
Wiping with the apron around her waist

My mother makes Creole bread
Great! Creole bread Aha!!!

Bob Marley

In this society
In this society of diversity
Cronyism and poverty
Was born a man tall
Bob Marley
Trench town boy
Of love, war and envy
He stood up for you
Stood up for me
Amongst the jealousy
Oh Lord Jah Lord
He love the brotherhood
Fast to the rock he stood
Singing redemption song
Get up stand up
Black man be free
Be proud
Be strong
Black or white
We all belong
White man why
Persecute the dread
Oh Jah me no want bald head
Oh my brother life is possibility

Aliston D. Crawford © 08/29/19

Them want me to cut my hair
Them want all of my locks to disappear
Don't think this is funny
For ever since I was a pikni
I have been growing my locks you know
Now my mother and my father
My sister and my grand ma
We are on the Channel 5 news
Stop this abuse! Stop this Abuse!
Sign the petition Keep your hand steady
Can't force the pikni to grow up until
The pikni is ready
Don't think this is funny
Don't think this is funny
You think this is funny?

Aliston D. Crawford © 08/29/19

Ah no wahn mash yuh carn
But wih cud feel dih pinch
Fuh true
So So fiyah bun
Pipple frayd fuh ton
Wih disyah fiyah bun
Rioters dem on dih run
So close yuh shap doh
Hide away yuh tv set
But no close yuh ears
Fuh dih deal not set yet
Baptize mih wid watah
Yuh revarent ministah
Baptize mih wid watah
Baptize mih wid watah
Yuh revarent ministah
Baptize mih wid watah
But no charge mih no income tax
No mek mih baptize yuh
Wid fiyah soon as you
Get back
One iguana tail cut off
Ena dih drayn leh down
Dis iguana caan't shake
Breggin
Dih city no have no fun
Wid disyah fiyah bun

Aliston D. Crawford © 1981

No Segregation

Why why dih pikney gwine bawl
Hungry belly no know no segregation
Blackman why yuh dih kipp yuhself so
Hungry belly no know no segregation
Why why dih pikney gwine bawl
Hungry belly no know no segregation
When yuh need yuh beg and beg
When yuh get, yuh could buy dih leg
Hungry belly no know no segregation
Black man no kipp yuhself so
Yuh have, but yuh need a little more
Why, "Why" dih pikney gwine bawl
Hungry belly no know no segregation
Crocus bag can't stand up when e empty
Crocus bag dah yuh mental not yuh belly

Chorus:
Bet yuh tink dah lie - come peep sih
If yuh tink dem sly - come peep sih
Bet yuh tink dah lie - come peep sih
If yuh tink dem sly - come peep sih

Bridge:
Old-fashion, like old fashion
Like old-fashion dah cuss wud
Old-fashion, like old fashion
Like old-fashion dah cuss wud
Just remembah dat old one bring new

Verse:
But dem seh Creole man
Hih no get exposure
Get exposure, man hih belly ton ovah
Cultivate him while hih young
Plant a seed in dih ground
Yuh can't push him down
Come try like hell
You'll try like hell
Yuh nevah push him down

Chorus:
Bet yuh tink dah lie - come peep sih
When yuh tink dem sly - come peep sih
Bet yuh tink dah lie - come peep sih
When yuh tink dah lie - come peep sih

© Aliston D. Crawford

Oh what a sight of dark
Cause yuh such a fright
Senseh black bone fowl
Fih go mek obeah
Okay yuh eyes get bright
Wih yuh jaw lock tight
And yuh skin roasting wid fevah
Senseh flesh dem slap pan yuh foot
Release yuh jaw mek yuh leap
Man yuh cure is ovah

It is the system
It is the system
Can't we change them
Run them from their street-pipe shower
Come bwai just sing dis song
Sing along
Sing dis song merry like a lark
In disyah taxi park

Singing two little candle
Red green and gold bangle
Children still looking out
Fuh Santa Claus
In the month of July
Brown skin baby fuh the
Clayre skin lady must
Be a shallie
Sing two little candle

Qualifications

What qualifies the worth of a man?
Not how tall he stands but how low he bends
To stretch out a hand to another
To his native land
What qualifies the worth of a man
Or the orange then
Not only the tree but the fruit there be
The orange to taste or it's juice to waste
Or the man set free

Aliston D. Crawford © May 11th 1981

With so much her dedication
She chooses the only solution
The Door! The Door!
She leaves- She leaves
She lives! Oh! Oh! Oh!
Its not the way we are making love
Its not the way we are making love
It was never the way nor was it
The reason
She was waiting too long
Don't know what she believes
Or if she is concern
As we judges her reflection
So unhappy is she
In God's perfection
Don't blame the world
Don't blame the world
You beautiful Girl
Life is guilty when
Life ignores the tragedy
Yes ! Yes! Yes!
Sweet is the rose
And prickle thorn
Pretty and illusive is the Swallow
That mocks the snow
After laughter defaces
The mountain side
Swallow! Swallow Fly
Screams of winter
Homeless and dying

The Turtle And The Snail

A country is a people
On a snail
That slowly glides over the rough
Over the smooth edges
By slimy belly
Among the wail
A country a symbol
Of the turtle and the snail
Both with harden shells
To hide from the hard the mean the tough
Always forward the turtle
Wins the race
Wins a little faster than the snail's pace
A country is a people
Living for the land
Living off the land
Willing with a hand to render
A mind to appreciate
The turtle and the snail
The trees they grow
From dawn to dust
But never in a day
It's majestic glow I trust
To bear the fruit
To show a flower
It's path and time
Is written by the turtle
And the Snail

Aliston D. Crawford © April 1981

Two Siding

Dah just two siding
Dah just two siding
Place to windward
Dah just two siding
Dah just two siding
Place to windward
Ah have a lake beneath mih feet
Fuh when ah feel like bathe or brush mih teeth
Man dah just two siding
No sand fly caant bite mih
When dih wind dih blow blow blow
Ah gat it made enah mih shade
Ah gat it made
No massah caan't drive mih
Cause ah no wan go oh no
Ah got it made, ah got mih shade
With no foreign aide

© *Aliston D. Crawford*

An oasis in sleep, await that aching foot
To trod on the place
Where little is yours to keep
Dreams of better
In spite of the shade of diversity
Elite or bourgeois
Realize man is man
Made to stand tall or not at all

© Aliston D. Crawford

Wih gat sappadilly
Bwai yu still no know yu roots
Baasley seed and vervine juice
Fih mek yuh see
How sweet Belize
Jelly-Jelly-Jelly-Jelly
Dah weh hih deh sah
Jelly-Jelly-Jelly-Jelly
Dah weh hih deh sah
Rite enah dih cowfoot soup ma
Gimme one dorey
Mek mih paddle up stream
Gwine go check mih graama
If fry plantain dih spoil
No blame dih cuknot oil
Yu haadah head

Aliston D. Crawford © 1980

All The Flowers

All the Flowers
And their perfume
Sun lit reflection
In beauty array
In love I swear
Attempt to fill the void
Of your absence
Wind why rustling
The leaves like
Diamonds glistening
Across the lagoon
Brilliant stirring
Yet again the memory
To echo in my brain
In time I know
I will be with you once again
As I heal as I begin
Again to trust
To walk in faith
For indeed I must
All the flowers
In joy for you

Aliston D. Crawford © 08/18/19

God's woman embracing His plan
Unafraid unapologetic unashamed
It is who I am
Yes! fertile ground
Not a rocky pathway
Nor a tumultuous sea
But a quiet stream
It is who I am
A woman
It is what I do
I influence change
I nurture character
It is who I am

Aliston D. Crawford © 09/02/19

Even though I coward out
Did not keep my word

Aliston D. Crawford © 08/30/19

Hand in hand together
To sleep in your arms again
Secure that you are my trusted friend
When I walk alone my forever ends
Like separate worlds are separate beds
Free! The torment of the child's head
When I walk alone I know my own
So I stay to seek my gain
When I walk alone I die! So afraid
You see
I want to run together with you
Share the burden of life together with you
Light the fire of passion - Of zeal - Of purpose
Of disappointment, Of achievement together with you
Yes! Come to me
Come cry in my arms
Laugh in my arms
Be angry in my arms
Dance in my arms
Dream in my arms
Hope in my arms
Love in my arms
Sleep in my arms
If possible Die in my arms
To live a smile of no regrets
To give a legacy of love
A legacy of Faith in Jesus Christ
COME

Aliston D.Crawford © 08/30/19

To Rise

Be slow to speak

Be quick to listen

Compliment before you criticize

There is place where to compromise

Help him, Help her to grow wings

Dad you help us to rise

Its all about you Jesus

Tell me what you intend to see

Its all about your plan

Lord reveal it to me

The seasons of life will come and will go

Your love Lord is constant so well do I know

It keeps me from falling your hand is secure

Compassion not failing your heart my open door

My good is your purpose

Faith arising in me to walk on water

To see you beckoning to me

As baby steps I take You celebrate my victory

Be slow to speak

Be quick to listen

Compliment before you criticize

There is a place where to compromise

Help him, help her to grow wings

Dad you help us to rise

Aliston D.Crawford©08/30/19

Back Ah Bush

Chorus:
Mih gwine gwine
Mih gwine back ah bush
Mih gwine gwine
Mih gwine back ah bush

Verse 1:
Going back ah bush one day
Going man fih haliday
Riding pan ah platform truck
Man mih nevah know mih luck
Dat dih wari dem cud smell so baad
But the carasow dem black like tar
And dih quaum dem get frighten
When dih crukrico start to bawl
And dih pyam -pyam dem gossip so much
Like mih sistah round she old scrub board
Oh mih nevah know sah
Bwai mih nevah know sah
Oh mih nevah know sah
Dat mih gwine back ah bush fih stay

Chorus:
Mih gwine gwine
Mih gwine back ah bush
Mih gwine gwine
Mih gwine back ah bush

But yuh mind pan dih tambran twig
Oh mih nevah know sah
Bread kind grow pan maamy tree
Oh mih nevah know sah
Mih eye open big fih sih
A hill call Vietman
And Wakahmaiyo no run so calm
Oh mih nevah know sah
Bwai mih nevah know sah
Oh mih nevah know sah
Dat mih gwine back ah bush fih stay

©Aliston D. Crawford

So yuh spend plenty money
Just fih keep out dih weddah
Buy yuh rabbit skin

Chorus:
Me seh fuh Kongoh Bud
Keep yuh wing dry
Kongoh fuh go weh
Me seh fuh Kongoh Bud
Kongoh fuh go deh
Weh yuh can fly
Kemo Kemo
Ane-he Dangriga
Kemo Kemo
Ane-he Punta Gorda
Kemo Kemo
Ane-he Belize City
Kemo Kemo
Ane-he Corozal

Verse:3
Ah seh dih scene's Kaliedoscopic
Here in dih tropics
Cucnot trees dih lean
So drop on in fuh a visit
Man yuh jus have fuh like it
Sunset are tangerine

Belizean Love Song

I will sing of blue skies
I will sing a love song
I will watch the birds fly
Feel the breeze blow strong
And sing to you
A Belizean Love song

I'll be near the pine trees
Hear the waters on the reef
Dancing Calypso and reggae Music
Under moonlight on the cayes
And sing to you the love song
When it is time to leave

You may go but you must come back
You may go but you must come back
You may go but you must come back
My heart is aching for the love of you
And the cucknot watah is a special treat
With fine conch fritters and lobster to eat
Drink and eat have lots of fun
Dance all night until the morning sun

You may go but you must come back
You may go but you must come back
You may go but you must come back
For to be gone a day seems a year or two

Drums of Belize

Drums of Belize
Sounding up dih dead
For love of freedom
For which dey Bled
Such audacity
This neighbor hungry
For dis place
Wid threats a studih- ting
Dah front a mih face
Bring out yuh shot gun
Dis dah no play
Bring out yuh warisama
Mek none get wey

Chorus:
Stand up people
Don't you buckle at the knee
Dis dah no punta dancing
You can do data with ease
Shout it out- shout it out
Belize dah fuh we
Nevah fear to get bruise
You nevah can loose
To fight to fight
For what you know is right

Look at the pine trees
Fresh flowing streams
Blue Blue waatah

Pressing on in liberty
When one fuh all
And one one mek three
We are small dah true
But a world will see

Chorus and fade:
Stand up people
Don't you buckle at the knee
Dis dah no punta dancing
You can do data with ease
Shout it out- shout it out
Belize dah fuh we
Nevah fear to get bruise
You nevah can loose
To fight to fight
For what you know is right

Aliston D.Crawford © 1978

Cause it overflows
This world cannot restrain it
We've got to let it go
It's faking
It's faking it's aching
Oh Oh Oh not giving back
Relating
Say thank you
Say thank you
Let His love flow
From the inside out
All the joy it gives
To freely give out
Let your kindness show
To all that's about
Loving you from the inside out
Loving you from the inside out
We can't keep it all
Let it overflow
In the kindness that you show
Come on let it go
It's faking
It's taking
Oh oh oh not giving back
Relating
Say thank you
Say thank you

Aliston D.Crawford © 10/12/16

Mr. Owl

How are you wise Mr. Owl Mr. Owl
I'm most quiet of the flying fowl
I flap my wings without a sound
My head is on swivel spinning round and round
Wisdom sees in the dark Who whoo who who who who who
With eyes wide open
Wisdom sees very clear who whoo who who who who who
Know when the danger is near
How are you wise Mr. Owl Mr. Owl
I'm most quiet of the flying fowl
I flap my wings without a sound
My head is on a swivel spinning round and round
Wisdom sees in the dark Who whoo who who who who who
With eyes wide open
Wisdom sees very clear Who whoo who who who who who
Knows when the answer is here

Aliston D. Crawford © 08/19/17

Come my brother we can relate
Commit to love
Above all else
In pleasure or in pain
Commit to love
In spite of the preacher
Drowning out the message
For personal gain
Sheet music
You done recorded my song
Now be careful
For the wind can blow you away
To be trampled on the street
Sheet music
Then the rhythm would be all wrong
In the motorcade that is passing
The trumpet sound
As running feet flees the parade

Aliston D. Crawford © 02/25/80

So I'll buy my paint
I deface their walls
For the cry in my heart
They don't hear at all
This crack is no joke
Yet it soothes my pain
Whether in the pipe
Or up my vein
Mommas into tv screen
Daddy is never seen
I color my hair
Yellow-yellow- yellow and pink
Where are your eye-eye-eyes
Why aren't you watching me
Lord oh Lord!
What happen to the children
They've taken up guns
Shooting other children
Lord oh Lord!
What happen to the children
They've taken up guns
Shooting other children
Am I the vendor that sold my daughter
This boy of anger?
Mommas into tv screen
Daddy is never seen
I color my hair
Yellow-yellow- yellow and pink
Where are your eye-eye-eyes
Why aren't you watching me?

Aliston D. Crawford © 08-29-19

Is a rich man
Bless with the house and land
Another is a poor man
Eating from the garbage can
You could be me
Even though your steeples are tall
And my thatch is low
You could be me
As your spirit cries to God
But your soul doesn't seem to know
Sitting in a corner
Sleeping at the bus stop
The wind is in my hair
You could be me
Sitting in the corner
Sleeping at the bus stop
The picture of despair
Don't you hear me
Crying
Don't you see me
Lying there
Don't you hear me
Crying
I've been wounded
I've been wounded
I've been wounded
In the house of my friend

Aliston D. Crawford © 08/29/19

PAINT & LEATHER
— *Caribbean Life* —

Aliston D.Crawford

Today I will be meeting my dad; or should I say, my father? I am perplexed about what I should call him. I am meeting him for the "first" time. The reason I put first in quotations is there is a shadow amongst the cobwebs of my memory.

Somewhere there is the recall of loud screaming and of door slamming and of the discourse about a brother at Listowell Boys' School. Apart from these associations that I try to bury, I do not remember anything about my father.

Currently, we are living in Belize City on Regent Street West, near East Canal, across from Georgie August Meat Shop. Along with the smell of sewage when the wind shifts, I have the additional unpleasant duty to report on a stepfather whom I utterly despise. It is hard living near the canal which doubles as the regulator of waste levels and the disposal unit of the open sewer when the tide rise and fall. Life is ever more stress filled because of this complete stranger, sleeping in my mother's bed, but one who is demanding respect without any real effort at a relationship on his part. He acts as he came pre-packaged with all the various colors of entitlement as leader of the pack, as the alpha dog.

Before you think that I am being too harsh, let me explain my Belize of the early nineteen fifties. We are a people just recently removed from slavery, but still under the thumb of our colonial masters. We are a male-dominated society where women's rights are not even a word. It is completely

Somehow, even at this tender age of five, I knew that a relationship so intimate and without a marriage license was not accepted by God. I knew the privilege this man was taking were not in agreement with any of us boys. My mom never consulted with any of us. She never told us why our father was missing. When the stepfather came we were simply told his name and that he would be staying with us.

We are meeting our father today. My brother and I. He is the brother that I followed in childbirth. We are about eighteen months apart and inseparable. We are meeting our dad today. My oldest brother is at reform school and my younger brother is the son of my stepfather. As I said before there are four of us. Three brothers are sons of my father and my youngest, well you know. I would discover later that my father had a son before he met my mother, but that is for a different story.

Today the arrangement is to meet him at noon, near the foot of the swing bridge, in front of Central Drug Store, at the beginning of Albert Street. We would meet him on the afternoon lunch break, on our way back home from school.

We went to Wesley Primary School, located on Albert Street. My teacher was Mrs. Frazier and she was loved by most of us. Sometimes she could be a bit scary but most of the time she was nice. I loved going to school. I loved having my brother with me. We could get into trouble together. Not intentional but just by being curious. We would sometime stop to gaze in the store window at Brodies or Romac's or Sikaffy. We would stare in shop windows all the while with nervous glances over our shoulders. We had to be alert. Our stepfather had assigned a job for himself and he monitored us constantly, on our way to school or on our way home from school. If by chance he saw us stopping at a store window, we would have to give an account as

This morning there was no cheese but we had butter and Creole bread. After, I went to the corner of the room where we slept and gathered by slate and pencil. Yes, a slate was what we used in schools and not paper or notebook. This was a tablet made of slate and we use this to write and record by scratching on the surface with a stone stylus. I placed my tablet in my bag and slipped on my short pants.

Most days we go to school barefoot, but today I am meeting my father. I got to look my best. I grabbed my paint and leather shoes and forced them unto my feet. They are a bit dry and stiff from being in the corner of the room in ninety-five plus degree heat. They were tar-black and shiny-looking and very hot when in the sun. These were my only pair and now they were hurting my feet. My feet began to sweat from the heat and the shoes got a bit loose from the moisture. My attention is not on the shoes on my feet. I am meeting my Dad!

I so much want him to see me and I so much want to ask him why I am just now meeting him. Why am I being subjected to this traumatic experience with a stepfather and what is he going to do about it. I had all my questions all ready for him. I would ask my father why he allowed such a life for his children and also why did my mother sit outside the room and did nothing but cry, when this monster slapped this four-year-old boy so hard, that he lost two of his upper front teeth and the two of his lower. Mom removed the two lower the following morning. I would ask my father why this had happened to me. I would ask my father if it is true that this man who is now my stepfather was once a young man whom he trusted and who in fact betrayed him and made off with my mom, his wife. I would ask him how did he allow this to happen to him and then to us his children. Why did he not fight to take us with him? Why did he abandon us? Was not his duty as a father to protect us.

Our lines were all tangled up. I had quite a task on my hand and was not quite happy with the responsibility but I kept at it. After all, we had decided to take on the challenge of paddling to the buoy and considering the other option of paddling, I decided that my task was the easiest.

We had gotten up just as the city was stirring and made our way to Central Market. There we "borrowed" my uncle dory that was tied up next to his fishing boat. He was in for the day and would not be going out to sea until the following day. We would bring it back in time. He would never know that it was gone.

Leaving the city market and paddling in front of the Bayview Hotel, we kept our dory close to the shoreline until we neared the governor's house and Bird's Isle. We then headed out across the open water. It was like skating on ice. The sea was so quiet until the minnow got eaten up.

I looked up from my task of unraveling the lines. I could not see the shape of the buoy on the horizon. We still had some ways to go.

The buoy was about two miles from the shoreline and we were told that the mackerel always swam pass this lane of current in the sea. It was a great spot. We would surely get some fish at this location.

The sound of the paddle hitting the water and the swishing sound as the dory glided over the water was all the effects this morning except for the occasional squawking of the seagull overhead. I guess the smell of raw conch in the bottom of the dory had alerted the bird. We would be using conch bits to bait our hooks. I looked at the two gallons of water and hope we had brought enough. It could be hot out here in the open.

Nuthun wrang wid dih bait bwai. Yuh haffe to have patience if you wan ketch anything Al. Yu dih bring up dih line too quick. Yuh have fuh wait till dih fish swalla before yuh jerk on yuh line bwai. Me mih tink yuh cud fish.

The day is going to be long with Walla and Seven-finger pulling in their fish. After about two hours and two little grunts to show, I am getting a look of disappointment from my friends. Now when uncle and I went out to fish it was a different story. I would know exactly what to do.

Uncle Aris stood about six feet four inches with a barrel chest and twenty inches of biceps. Aris is short for Aristotle. He had a smile like the Colgate commercial and a frame that filled the doorway whenever he would stop by our home. Uncle never came empty handed. We would all be happy campers around a fifteen-pound red snapper baked in the oven with mom's special Belizean spices. We loved our Uncle Aris. He loved to read the bible and play the guitar. He only knew four chords and played and sang everything in those same four chords.

He was the youngest of my mom's two brothers. He would always be checking up on his sister and her four boys. Mom was a single mother and had her hands full with us tugging at her every which way.

Buddi how dem pikney dih behave gyal?

Aris bwai wih dih manage yu noh

Aris, maybe yuh cud tek Al out wih you one day fishing? Hih seh he wan larn fuh sail yu boat.

Bwai yuh wah com wih mih? Yes Uncle

this fire and brimstone preacher. There would the noise the traffic his voice would shouting above the clammer. Get yuh Kingfish! Fresh Mackerel four dalla ah pound! Repent! Yuh have fuh change yuh ways mih bredda, mih sistah! Come to Jesus! He loves yuh!

No matter how hot the day or how much the people pushed my uncle's response was that sparkling colgate smile. He was like this buoy bobbing up and down yet anchored firmly on the seabed, steady, dependable.

I felt the massive tug that yanked me off my seat and landed me in the dory. My hand became inflamed as I desperately tried to keep the nylon rapped around the palm of my hand. I shouted at Walla and George. Bwai! Bwai! Ah, gat something! Hih big! Yuh betta help me! The dory is rocking back and forth in all the excitement. Gyann some slack bwai, den pull ah ein! I am doing all I can to tire out this flash of gray I see outlined as I am reeling it in. As it got near and its head is coming up, I see this monster with a long flat sword like weapon armed with teeth on both sides. Its eyes were a pearcing glare of anger on both sides of it's flat, gray head. I jumbed back to the rear of the dory and shouted. Kill it! Tek it! Tek it!

I felt someone pushing me back and grabbing the nylon and began to tug of the monster. If was Seven-finger George. Beside him is Walla. We are now all in the dory and are being towed by this fish. Finally, with all the excitement, it tired out and George continued to pull it in. Again I saw the two-edge sword and glaring rows of teeth, as Walla began to wack it on its head with the paddle. He rendered it lifeless and we pulled it into the dory. We had our first look at the six-foot long saw-fish. We were ready to go home. As we became aware of our surroundings, we notice had been taken some distance from our perch on the buoy.

www.ingramcontent.com/pod-product-compliance
Lightning Source LLC
Chambersburg PA
CBHW020120180726
47992CB00019B/1413